Kabuki Gift

An Original Play

Kabuki Gift

An Original Play

by Douglas Love

HarperCollins*Publishers*

1   2   3   4   5   6   7   8   9   10

❖

First Edition

For my most honorable friends Gretta, Sharon,
Jamie, Todd, and Norrice

Introduction

The first time I stepped inside a theater, I thought that it was the most magical place in the world. I went with my class to see a show at the performing arts center in my town. It was a musical for children produced by a professional company of actors. I was immediately captivated. Right there in front of me, performers were singing and dancing and telling a story—live! It seemed that they were talking directly to me, and I was completely enthralled with the characters and their adventures. The sets and costumes weren't fancy or extravagant, but this made me even more involved in the production. I was able to use my imagination to pick up where the limitations of the sets and costumes left off. This first production was my introduction to the world of theater.

You are about to embark on an exciting adventure. Planning, rehearsing, and staging a play can be a fun and satisfying experience. It's up to you to make your play the best it can be. The written script is only the beginning. It is meant to be used like a map, a route that guides you through the story.

Because actors in a play are right in front of an audience (not up on a movie screen or inside a television), anything can happen, and it usually does. Scenery may fall over, people may say the wrong lines at the wrong time or forget their lines altogether. When these mistakes happen, the actors can't stop and start over. In the theater, they go right on and try to get back on track with as much ease as possible. This is the challenge of live theater. The feeling that *anything can happen* keeps everyone on their toes.

While working on your production, don't be discouraged if you feel that you don't have the exact prop or costume that the play calls for. If the stage directions ask for a couch in a certain scene, there is no rule that says you can't use a bench, or a chair, or nothing at all instead. You should decide what you think is important to include. Some of the best plays have no props or stage settings at all. The audience has to use its imagination, which can be a lot of fun.

It is almost always helpful to have someone serve as the director of the play, whether you are performing in your school or your backyard. This person will help make decisions about the direction your production takes: Will everyone wear costumes? Will you make a set? Who will play which character? He or she may also designate certain parts of the stage to be different places where the action takes place. The director should also help everyone working on the play realize that theater is a collaborative art. This means that the talents of a lot of people come together to create one exciting production that everyone can be proud of because everyone helped to create it.

Performers have a special task in the play. When you know what role you will play, the next step is to develop your character. This is achieved by asking yourself a lot of questions: If I was this person (or animal), how would I walk? How would I stand? How would I speak? What would I wear? Whom do I like in the play? Whom don't I like? What do I want to do in the play? You can and should ask yourself these and more questions about your character. Then, you have to answer these questions and make some decisions. If you are playing an old man, you might decide to stand hunched over and walk with a cane. You may choose to have a gravelly voice and tattered clothes. You may discover while reading the play that you are a rich old man who doesn't spend any of his money, and you are afraid that everyone is trying to steal it.

The answers and decisions that you make about your character are guideposts on your journey. It's okay to change your mind if something isn't working. None of the choices that you make for your character are wrong. Experiment! That's what rehearsals are for. Refer to the performance tips before each play for some suggestions.

Rehearsal is extremely important if you plan to perform your play for an audience. Some theater directors and actors believe that you should rehearse one hour for every minute that you are onstage. Some of that rehearsal time can be spent on your own, memorizing your lines. Different people memorize lines differently, but all techniques have one thing in common— repetition. Go over and over and over your lines until you can say them without looking at the script. Some people sit alone reading their lines again and again until they can say them from memory. Others read their lines into a tape recorder and listen to the tape over and over. Or ask a friend or someone in your family to "hold book." This means that they read the line that comes before yours and then you say your line.

Rehearsal is also the time to decide on your blocking, or the physical action of the play. Who does what, when? If everything is planned before the performance, you'll feel more secure, and the audience will be able to follow the story more easily.

When planning your blocking, remember that you are performing for an audience that needs to see what is going on to follow the story of the play. Important action should take place closer to the audience. Try to face the audience as much as possible; this allows them to see your facial expressions and hear you better.

Whether you will be performing on your school stage, in your classroom, or at home, feel free to make changes to make the play work for you, and use them as a jumping off point into the unlimited world of your own creativity and imagination.

About *Kabuki Gift*

Kabuki Gift is written to be performed in the Kabuki theater style, mainly in its appearance and in its themes of honor and humor. Kabuki is a Japanese theater form that is a combination of music, movement, theater, and pantomime. In Japan, Kabuki theater is traditionally performed only by men. Female characters are played by male actors. This is because when Kabuki theater originated, it was believed that performing was not a respectable or ladylike activity for women. However, *Kabuki Gift* is meant to be performed by male and female actors.

Written with the utmost respect for Japanese culture, *Kabuki Gift* combines the beauty of the Kabuki theater form with some American humor to create a multicultural, fun experience for both performers and audience.

The Characters

Portraying a character who is very different from you can be a challenge. In *Kabuki Gift*, there is the added difficulty of portraying a different culture and historical period. In order for actors to create the most believable and realistic performance possible, they often must research the time and place in which the characters lived. The library is an excellent place to find this information.

Tu-bah is the exalted wise elder of the region. He speaks in a slow, steady manner with a deep voice and is respected by all of the characters in the play. Every time his name is mentioned, all the characters onstage bow respectfully. He is an old man, and might have a beard.

Rum-ti is the elected official of the people. He will do anything to please the citizens of the town, including giving his daughter's hand in marriage to Bah-low, the warrior from the next town, to keep the peace in the region.

Pum-ti is the wife of Rum-ti. She appears faithfully beside her husband at all official ceremonies. She is in charge of all the preparations for her daughter's wedding and is very concerned about doing what is honorable.

Ti-ti is the daughter of Rum-ti and Pum-ti. She is very upset about the wedding arrangement that her father has made. She is torn between her dedication to her family honor and her love for Roe-nye.

Chi is the servant for Rum-ti and his family.

May-nye is a kindhearted doctor who helps the poor and does not charge them for his services. As a result, he too is very poor and owes money to Yen-noh, a mean, stingy rich man.

Qua-nye is the wife of May-nye. She wishes that her husband would make some money. She is very nervous and easily excited.

Roe-nye is the son of May-nye and Qua-nye, and he is in love with Ti-ti. He is concerned with proving his worthiness to Ti-ti's father in the hope that he will win the right to marry her.

Fan-tu is a baker whose only day off is Wednesday. When awakened from her Wednesday sleep, she is very cranky. She does, however, have a soft spot in her heart for true love.

Piti-pan and **Opo-ran** are craftspeople who work very hard to sell their goods.

Bah-low is a warrior from the next town who is brought in to marry Ti-ti. Everyone thinks that he is mean and rough when in fact he is very sensitive and kind.

8

Tuh-noh is the daughter of Yen-noh and is crazy about sushi. She loves it! She meets Roe-nye and offers to help him find his gift for Ti-ti. They become good friends, and she learns about the many different ways that one person can care about another.

Yen-noh is an old man who is very rich and tight with his money. He has a secret plan to marry off his daughter Tuh-noh to May-nye's son, Roe-nye. His sushi bills are too high.

Day-sol is a traveling bamboo trader. She works hard and travels the region on foot. She is very tired, yet she tries to be helpful.

Koh is Day-sol's assistant, who is also weary from the road and complains about their working conditions. Koh can be a male or female character.

The Whistling Wind Women are mysterious keepers of the secret of love. They guard it and refuse to share it. They seem angry and dangerous.

Bo is the servant to the Whistling Wind Women. Bo is a little slow and serves the Wind Women faithfully. Bo can be a male or female character.

Roe-mal is the official town pessimist. He always thinks that the worst will happen.

Koh-mie is the official town optimist. She can always spot the good in every situation.

Taffle-si was appointed mayor of the town by Tu-bah.

Aye, Goh, Lah, and **Fie** are the children of Taffle-si. They are restless, hungry, and tired and would much rather be playing games than going to official ceremonies with their father.

Sets and Props

Much of the set in a traditional Kabuki play is made of cutout and painted pieces of wood that represent trees, rocks, and other objects. There are often painted drops hanging at the back of the stage and ornate curtains called *maku*, usually pulled from one side of the stage to the other.

In *Kabuki Gift*, the setting can remain constant throughout the play. The scenery should reflect the Japanese culture expressed in the play. You may create Japanese screens, or banners with Japanese words written on them. Or you may want to hang a beautiful Japanese kimono or robe by putting a broomstick through the sleeves.

Be creative in the way you decorate your Kabuki stage. Remember that the Kabuki style is simple and elegant. Don't clutter the stage with too many objects. Your actors will need space to move around.

You can put on *Kabuki Gift* anywhere there's a bit of room. The most important thing to do in a space that is not a real stage is to define your acting area. This means you can decide what is onstage and what is offstage. You can use a clothesline to hang a curtain or a blanket for a backdrop. Designate a backstage area where actors cannot be seen by the audience.

Remember, limited resources don't have to be a handicap. Think of them as a challenge to your creativity and let your imagination take over.

Costumes and Makeup

It's fun to pretend that you are someone else. When you add the element of costume and you begin to look like some other character and not like yourself, the fun really begins.

Traditional Kabuki costumes, or *isho*, are very colorful and ornate. All Kabuki costumes are worn in layers. All actors wear an under and outer *kimono* (robe), over which may be worn additional robes and jackets. If you don't have a kimono, use layers of sheets and other robes that you may already have to create a layered, drapery look.

One of the most noticeable elements of Kabuki theater is the special makeup. Kabuki makeup is called *kesho*. Each traditional Kabuki role has a set style of makeup. Most traditional makeup has a base of white. It is believed that the white base hides the real person who is the actor and allows the character to come out.

Female characters usually have high black eyebrows, a thin red line under their eyes, and delicate red lips, all on top of the white base. Male characters usually have larger black eyebrows and full red lips, also on the white base. Warriors usually have thick, sweeping black brows and face lines with red highlights.

As with all the visual elements of Kabuki theater, the traditional makeup, although mostly white, black, red, and blue, is bold and stylized.

Cast

Tu-bah, exalted wise elder
Rum-ti, elected official of the people
Pum-ti, his wife
Ti-ti, their daughter
Chi, their servant
May-nye, a doctor
Qua-nye, his wife
Roe-nye, their son
Fan-tu, a baker
Piti-pan, a craftsperson
Opo-ran, a tailor
Yen-noh, a miser
Tuh-noh, his sushi-loving daughter
Bah-low, a warrior
Whistling Wind Woman #1
Whistling Wind Woman #2
Whistling Wind Woman #3
Bo, their attendant
Day-sol, a traveling bamboo trader
Koh, her assistant
Roe-mal, the town cynic

Koh-mie, the town optimist

Taffle-si, appointed mayor*

Aye, Goh, Lah, and Fie, his children*

*These characters are omitted when working with the smaller cast (eight actors).

Optional Smaller Cast

Actor 1—Roe-nye

Actor 2—Tuh-noh, Chi, Piti-pan

Actor 3—Bah-low, Yen-noh, Koh

Actor 4—Ti-ti, Fan-tu, Wind Woman #3

Actor 5—May-nye, Roe-mal

Actor 6—Rum-ti, Bo, Opo-ran

Actor 7—Pum-ti, Tu-bah, Day-sol, Wind Woman #2

Actor 8—Qua-nye, Wind Woman #1, Koh-mie

★*If you have only eight actors, Scene 1 should start with the entrance of the* COMPANY *(page 17). Scene 2 should be skipped.*

Setting

Scene 1: The town square
Scene 2: The town square
Scene 3: The house of Tu-bah
Scene 4: A bakery
Scene 5: A craft-and-tailor shop
Scene 6: The house of May-nye, Qua-nye,
and Roe-nye
Scene 7: The house of Rum-ti, Pum-ti, and Ti-ti
Scene 8: The road, just outside of town
Scene 9: The dwelling of the Whistling
Wind Women
Scene 10: The town square
Scene 11: The town square

Scene 1

★ *The town square. The mayor,* TAFFLE-SI, *and his four children have gathered in the town square. A raised platform sits centerstage.* TAFFLE-SI *and his children stand on the platform.*

Taffle-si *(to himself)*: Where is everyone?

Goh: I'm hungry.

Aye: I want to go home.

Lah: I'm bored!

Fie: When can we leave?

Taffle-si: Honorable children, do not whimper. Honorable children should obey the wishes of their parents.

Fie: What are your wishes, Father?

Taffle-si *(to himself)*: I thought that everyone would be early for such an event. I bet I know

16

where they are. They are all over at the house of Rum-ti. Rum-ti is, after all, the honorable elected official of the people, and I am just the appointed mayor. But I was appointed by the wise town elder, Tu-bah.

All four kids: Ah, Tu-bah, Tu-bah!

★ *Throughout the play, every time a character mentions the name TU-BAH, all the actors onstage bow with great respect.*

Lah: Papa, why are we here today for this celebration?

Taffle-si: This is the anniversary of our town's founding.

★ *The COMPANY (except ROE-NYE) enters and gathers around the central platform. As they enter, they bow to each other in greeting. RUM-TI, PUM-TI, and TI-TI step onto the platform. RUM-TI begins to address the crowd.*

Rum-ti: Welcome, everyone, to this great celebration. I know that I speak for my family when I say that the people of this town made it the honorable place that it is today and will create the honorable future of our town for our worthy children, as advised by Tu-bah.

All: Ah, Tu-bah, Tu-bah!

Ti-ti: Who is Tu-bah, Mother?

Pum-ti: He is the wisest man in the town.

Ti-ti: Where is he? Point him out to me.

Pum-ti: He is not here, my honorable child; he lives in the house near the bonsai grove. Shhh, your father is going to talk again.

Rum-ti: As elected official of the town, I would like to proceed with the fulfillment of my campaign promises. You will be happy to note that disposable chopsticks shall be outlawed in our worthy town. We have not the trees to spare for such a thing. "Wash and reuse," that is our new motto. *(Looking at his notes)* Number two . . . Our old motto . . . "Use it or lose it" . . . shall be officially replaced. . . . Number three . . .

★ *RUM-TI continues his speech silently as we hear the private conversations of people in the crowd.*

Those actors onstage not involved in the dialogue watch RUM-TI *as if he is still speaking.*

Roe-nye *(running on, to* MAY-NYE*)*: Father, am I late? Is she here?

May-nye *(pointing to* TI-TI*)*: She is up there next to her father.

Qua-nye *(to* ROE-NYE*)*: There's Yen-noh, that stingy miser! How I wish your father didn't owe him so much money. He is always hanging it over our heads.

Roe-nye: One day I will be very rich, Mother, and I will pay off all of Father's debts.

Qua-nye: Your father is most likely the only doctor who is losing money rather than making it!

May-nye: How can I charge the sick for my services? They are poor and need my help.

Qua-nye: We are poor, too!

Yen-noh *(walking over to* MAY-NYE *with his daughter,* TUH-NOH*)*: Hello, May-nye. I haven't

19

received your latest loan payment yet.

May-nye: I will have it for you Tuesday, I promise you, Yen-noh.

Yen-noh: I certainly hope so, May-nye. You know I don't mean to sound pushy—

Tuh-noh *(perking up)*: Sushi?

Yen-noh: No, dear, not sushi . . .

Tuh-noh: I love sushi! All kinds and shapes and colors and sizes!

Yen-noh: Yes, my daughter, I know. Come along now.

Tuh-noh: Where are we going? Will we have sushi there?

★ *YEN-NOH and TUH-NOH exit.*

★ *We hear RUM-TI again, as if he had been speaking all along.*

Rum-ti: . . . and as I promised, I will marry my

lovely daughter Ti-ti to the warrior Bah-low from the next town to maintain the peace!

Ti-ti *(alarmed)*: No, Father!

★ *ROE-NYE bravely comes forward.*

Roe-nye: No! Sir, you cannot give your daughter to the warrior Bah-low from the next town to keep the peace! I love your daughter and wish to marry her!

Rum-ti *(laughing)*: *You?* You are hardly worthy of my daughter. Besides, it is the will of the people that my daughter marry the warrior from the next town to keep the peace.

Ti-ti: No, Father! *(Runs off crying.)*

Pum-ti *(following her)*: Ti-ti, wait!

★ *Blackout*

Scene 2

★ *Same place, immediately following.* ROE-NYE *and the mayor's children are the only ones left onstage.*

Goh: Play the rhyming game with us, Roe-nye!

Roe-nye: My honorable heart is broken.

Lah: Broken!

Aye: Token!

★ *The children hold hands and skip around* ROE-NYE *in a circle.*

Roe-nye: I'm not playing the game! I am too sad!

Lah: Sad!

Aye: Bad!

Goh: Mad!

★ *The children circle again.*

Roe-nye: Honorable friends, my heart is as blue as the setting sun is orange.

Lah: Orange!

★ *The kids cannot rhyme that. They look perplexed.*

Aye: How can we help?

Roe-nye: What can I do to show Ti-ti's father that I am worthy of his daughter?

Lah: Tell him!

Roe-nye: I tried! He said it was the will of the people that Ti-ti marry the warrior Bah-low from the next town to keep the peace.

Fie: You need to show her father that you are worthy!

Lah: How can we show him?

Roe-nye: I can give Ti-ti a gift that would show her honorable father that I am worthy.

Aye: It would have to be a very honorable gift!

Roe-nye: I would be wise to ask the wisest man in the region what gift I should present Ti-ti to prove my worthiness.

Fie: Who is that?

Roe-nye: Tu-bah!

All: Ah, Tu-bah, Tu-bah!

★ *They all bow in respect for TU-BAH.*

★ *Blackout*

Scene 3

★ *The house of* TU-BAH. *TU-BAH stands centerstage, alone. He has an imposing presence. You may also portray* TU-BAH *as a mysterious voice with no actor onstage.*

Tu-bah: Enter, knowledge seeker!

★ *ROE-NYE enters, nervous.*

Roe-nye: Ah, Tu-bah, Tu-bah!

★ *ROE-NYE bows.*

Tu-bah: Sit!

★ *ROE-NYE sits.*

Roe-nye: Exalted wise elder, I must find a gift!

Tu-bah: A gift?

Roe-nye: Yes, your exaltedness!

Tu-bah: Who shall receive it, young son?

Roe-nye: It is for my intended, sir. Ti-ti, daughter of Rum-ti, the elected official of the people.

Tu-bah: And why a gift, young son? Is there to be a celebration?

Roe-nye: I hope there is to be a wedding—mine, to her!

Tu-bah: Do you love her, young son?

Roe-nye: With all my heart.

Tu-bah: And she you?

Roe-nye: Oh, yes! She told me so in her delicate manner.

Tu-bah: What troubles you then?

Roe-nye: Her father, your exalted, intends to marry his daughter to Bah-low, the warrior from the next town, to keep the peace.

Tu-bah: A marriage of convenience.

Roe-nye: I find it very inconvenient. That is why I must present her with a gift so exceptional that her father and everyone else in the town sees that I am most worthy of his daughter's hand in marriage.

Tu-bah: . . . and a gift shall prove this.

Roe-nye: Not just any gift—a very special and honorable gift. This is why I come to you, your exaltedness. I request your suggestion for the most honorable gift.

Tu-bah: There are many fine craftspeople in your town. Go to them and seek your gift. Maybe you will find something. Above all, follow your heart.

Roe-nye: I thank you, wise exalted elder. Ah, Tu-bah, Tu-bah. *(He bows.)*

★ *Blackout*

Scene 4

★ *The bake shop.* ROE-NYE *enters and calls to the baker.*

Roe-nye: Fan-tu! Are you here? *(Waits for an answer.)* Fan-tu! *(Waits again.)* Fan-tu!

★ FAN-TU *enters, obviously just awakened.*

Fan-tu *(yawning)*: What is it? What do you want?

Roe-nye: You are the finest baker in town! I come to you for a special sweet gift!

Fan-tu *(angrily)*: Do you not know what day it is!?

Roe-nye: I bid your forgiveness, honorable baker. In my excitement I do not know the day.

Fan-tu: It is Wednesday!

Roe-nye: And what is particular about Wednesday?

Fan-tu: It is my day off. I sleep Wednesdays! Oh, the inconvenience of paper walls.

Roe-nye: I am sorry to disrupt your sleep—but this is an emergency! I need a gift for Ti-ti to declare my worthiness to wed her!

Fan-tu: You love Ti-ti?

Roe-nye: With all my heart.

Fan-tu: Then I shall help you. I have a wonderful gift for you to give Ti-ti. I learned this from a Chinese baker. You can write her a fortune to place in a delicious cookie.

Roe-nye: I don't know how to write fortunes!

★ *FAN-TU starts to clap a beat and begins her chant.*

Fan-tu: It is easy. Just follow my lead!
You have the ability to know the higher truth!
Next full moon brings good luck!

★ *ROE-NYE has trouble keeping the beat.*

Roe-nye: *If your thumb is green—wash it again!*

29

★ *FAN-TU stops clapping and looks at ROE-NYE in disbelief. She decides to try again.*

Fan-tu: *A stranger comes to you from far away!*
Riches and joy to all who come this day!

★ *ROE-NYE is again off beat.*

Roe-nye: *It's a good time to clean your closet!*

Fan-tu: Maybe you should buy her a hat!

★ *Blackout*

Scene 5

★ *The craft-and-tailor shop.*

Roe-nye *(explaining his problem)*: So, you see my dilemma, worthy craftspeople. I must have a gift of great honorability.

Piti-pan: I've a ceramic duck emblazoned in gold.

Roe-nye: Does it fly?

Piti-pan: No, but the eye moves with remarkable naturalness.

Opo-ran: And I have a special scarf woven from the silk of eighty-nine worms that I cultivated myself. I kept them in a bamboo chest and hand fed them leaves! The fabric is smooth and the color a favorite of all the young girls of our town.

Roe-nye: All the young girls like it, do they?

Opo-ran: It is much sought after.

31

Roe-nye: I thank you for your suggestions, kind providers. I cannot give my love a bird that does not fly. My feelings for Ti-ti cannot be limited by ceramic and gold. And I cannot give her a scarf that has been viewed by many others, for our love has been a beautiful secret that is just for us. I must return to my home to ponder.

★ *ROE-NYE bows and exits.*

★ *Blackout*

Scene 6

★ *The home of* ROE-NYE. ROE-NYE *is speaking to his mother,* QUA-NYE.

Roe-nye: . . . and none of the gifts were right, Mother. They did not capture the spirit of my feelings.

Qua-nye: Where did you expect to get the money to pay for such a gift? You know that all of the money that Father makes must go to pay Yen-noh.

Roe-nye: Why does Father owe that awful man so much money?

Qua-nye: When your father finished his medical lessons, he had no money to purchase the necessary instruments to practice his profession.

Roe-nye: Why did he ask Yen-noh for the money?

Qua-nye: He is the richest man in the town.

★ MAY-NYE *rushes in, nervous.*

May-nye: Family! Has Yen-noh arrived yet? He said he'd arrive at two moons, and it is nearly three! It is not like that man to be late.

Qua-nye: Especially when he is coming for money.

May-nye: I do hope that he is in a more charitable mood than the one he was wearing at the celebration.

Qua-nye: You *do* have his money, don't you, May-nye?

May-nye: I fear not, dear wife!

Qua-nye: I thought you were to collect the medical fees today.

May-nye: I was, but when I went to call for my money, everyone seemed so poor and needy that I could not accept their payments.

Qua-nye: Let us only hope that Yen-noh has such a generous heart as yours.

★ *YEN-NOH enters with his daughter, TUH-NOH, who is eating sushi.*

Yen-noh: May-nye, I have come for my money!

34

May-nye *(very nervous)*: I can explain . . .

Yen-noh: Excuses! Excuses don't pay my sushi bills!

Tuh-noh *(still eating)*: Sushi!

Yen-noh: Yes, yes, dear daughter, eat your sushi. May-nye, I want to speak with you in private. We must come to a settlement of this debt.

May-nye: Very well. Roe-nye, entertain Tuh-noh.

★ *All exit except for* TUH-NOH *and* ROE-NYE.

★ TUH-NOH *sits down to give her full attention to her food.* ROE-NYE *attempts to make conversation.*

Roe-nye: Nice night.

★ TUH-NOH *doesn't react.*

Roe-nye: Sort of warm out.

★ TUH-NOH *doesn't react.*

Roe-nye: Is your food very good?

Tuh-noh *(realizing that he is speaking to her)*: It's

okay. *(She goes back to eating.)*

Roe-nye: You like sushi?

Tuh-noh *(perking up, she is always happy to talk about sushi)*: I LOVE sushi! It is the very best food there is! When I am eating sushi, I can rest assured that I am providing myself with the proteins and essential minerals that are the R.D.A.B.T.B.

Roe-nye: R.D.A.B.T.B.? What does that stand for?

Tuh-noh: Recommended Daily Allowance By Tu-bah.

★ *They bow.*

Both: Ah, Tu-bah, Tu-bah!

Roe-nye: You know Tu-bah?

Tuh-noh: I've met him on three occasions.

Roe-nye: I have met with him only once.

Tuh-noh: On the subject of nourishment?

Roe-nye: No. On the subject of love.

36

Tuh-noh: I love sushi!

Roe-nye: I love Ti-ti!

Tuh-noh: With rice and soy sauce?

Roe-nye: Ti-ti is not a food. She is the daughter of Rum-ti, the elected official of the people!

Tuh-noh: You love her?

Roe-nye: With all my heart. I wish to marry her!

Tuh-noh: I love sushi! But I do not wish to marry sushi. It must be different. I can see why you sought out the advice of Tu-bah.

Both *(bowing)*: Ah, Tu-bah, Tu-bah!

Roe-nye: I went to him for gift suggestions. You see, Ti-ti's father wishes that Ti-ti marry the warrior Bah-low from the next town to keep the peace in the region. Ti-ti doesn't love Bah-low. She loves me.

Tuh-noh: Does she love you like I love sushi or like you love her?

37

Roe-nye: Like I love her, I assume.

Tuh-noh: How can you be sure? Has she ever mentioned soy sauce in your presence?

Roe-nye: Of course not!

Tuh-noh: What is this gift for?

Roe-nye: To convince her father that I am worthy of his daughter's hand in marriage.

Tuh-noh: What will you buy her?

Roe-nye: That is just my problem. I have visited the fine craftspeople of our town, and I cannot find that which expresses what is in my heart.

Tuh-noh *(alarmed)*: What is in your heart?

Roe-nye: Love is in my heart! Tu-bah says that I should follow my heart!

Both *(bowing)*: Ah, Tu-bah, Tu-bah!

★ *We hear TU-BAH's voice from offstage.*

Tu-bah: Follow your heart! Follow your heart!

Tuh-noh: Maybe you should not limit yourself to the boundaries of this town. I know a bamboo trader who travels through the entire region. This trader could tell us where to find the perfect gift. Come!

★ *They exit.*

★ *MAY-NYE and YEN-NOH enter.*

Yen-noh: So it is settled. You will have my money by this time tomorrow or you will consent to have your son marry my daughter. *(YEN-NOH crosses downstage right to speak directly to the audience, without the other characters hearing.)* I do not need his money! This way I will marry off my daughter and someone else can pay to feed her!

★ *YEN-NOH exits.*

May-nye *(Crosses to the same downstage right spot to speak to the audience.)*: What shall I do? I have no money and my son is in love with Ti-ti!

★ *MAY-NYE exits.*

★ *Blackout*

Scene 7

★ *The house of* RUM-TI. PUM-TI *is altering* TI-TI's *wedding dress.* CHI, *a servant, is standing in the background, waiting.*

Pum-ti: It is the will of the people. You know how your father feels about the will of the people.

Ti-ti: But it is not my will, Mother. I do not love the warrior Bah-low from the next town. I love Roe-nye. He is the one I wish to marry. He is the one I love.

Pum-ti: Think of it as your civic duty . . .

Ti-ti: And if I deny my duty?

Pum-ti *(shocked)*: Ti-ti, that is a highly dishonorable thought.

Ti-ti: I am sorry, Mother. I am out of my head.

Pum-ti *(to her servant, CHI)*: Chi, please bring Ti-ti some tea.

Chi: Yes, ma'am.

Pum-ti: And Chi, please bring my cloak.

Chi: Yes, ma'am.

★ *CHI exits.*

Pum-ti: Ti-ti, I wish that it could be different—but it looks like you will be wearing this dress tomorrow as you wed the warrior Bah-low from the next town. Now, I am going to make the preparations.

★ *PUM-TI exits.*

★ *CHI enters with TI-TI's tea.*

Chi: Here is your tea. Drink it slowly. This is the last cup you will have before the marriage cup.

Ti-ti: The marriage cup?

Chi: Yes, you and Bah-low will drink from the same cup of tea to seal your marriage. The marriage is not legal until you share the tea.

Ti-ti: Then I do not want to drink tea! Take this away! With every sip I can only think that I am losing my one true love—Roe-nye. *(She sobs as the lights dim.)*

★ *Blackout*

Scene 8

★ *The road.* DAY-SOL *and* KOH *(the bamboo trader and her assistant) walk on. They are weary from walking. They stop to rest.*

Koh: How much longer is the walk? We must be approaching the next town.

Day-sol: It is over the next hill. It seems the closer the town becomes, the more my feet give way.

Koh: Each year these towns seem to get farther and farther apart.

Day-sol: Such is the life of a traveling bamboo trader.

Koh: Oh, shoot!

★ *They both sigh.*

★ TUH-NOH *and* ROE-NYE *enter calling after them.*

Tuh-noh: Day-sol! Day-sol! I am so glad that we caught up to you!

Day-sol: Ah, Tuh-noh, what a surprise. Your father didn't send you, did he? I promised that I would pay him back on the seventh moon!

Tuh-noh: No, no. I came because my friend needs your help.

Day-sol: I am very sorry, but we are not looking for another tradesperson. It is all I can do to support Koh and myself.

Roe-nye: I am not looking for a job. I am looking for a gift. A special gift to show that I am worthy to marry.

Day-sol: It is not our practice to act as present consultants.

Tuh-noh: He comes from Tu-bah!

All *(bowing)*: Ah, Tu-bah, Tu-bah!

Day-sol: Well, why didn't you say so in the first place? What is it you're looking for?

Roe-nye: I have been to many merchants and cannot find a gift that expresses that which is in my heart.

★ *We hear* TU-BAH's *voice from offstage.*

Tu-bah: Follow your heart. Follow your heart.

Day-sol: I know just the gift. But it is guarded.

Roe-nye *(determined)*: If it is the right gift, an entire army could not guard it from me.

Day-sol: It is guarded by three mysterious women and their equally mysterious attendant, Bo.

Roe-nye: What is it they guard?

Day-sol: The secret of love.

Roe-nye *(excited)*: If I were to give Ti-ti the secret of love, her father would have to let her marry me! Where are these women?

Day-sol: They are very mysterious. They may even be dangerous.

Roe-nye: I am not afraid. Are you afraid, Tuh-noh?

Tuh-noh *(afraid)*: Just how mysterious are these women?

Day-sol: Very mysterious! They are known as the Whistling Wind Women. Their voices whistle a mysterious song.

Roe-nye: Please, lead us to them!

★ *Blackout*

Scene 9

★ *The dwelling of the* WHISTLING WIND WOMEN. *The* WHISTLING WIND WOMEN *are whispering around a small box in the center of the stage. They perform their whistling dance. During the dance,* TUH-NOH *and* ROE-NYE *enter and hide in a corner upstage.* WIND WOMAN *#1 notices them and stops the dance.*

Wind Woman #1: What have we here? Are you intruders?

Roe-nye: Why, no. We were just passing through on our way to the next town.

Wind Woman #2 *(not believing them)*: Passing through?

Wind Woman #3: Our dwelling is not on the way to anywhere.

Wind Woman #2: I don't believe them.

Wind Woman #3: I say we must proceed with caution.

46

Bo: Would you like me to check them for hidden thoughts?

Wind Woman #1 *(pretending to be nice)*: That won't be necessary, Bo. These fine people are our guests. We must treat them with respect and welcome them to our dwelling.

Wind Woman #2: Welcome, dear guests.

Wind Woman #3: We are pleased that you could join us.

Wind Woman #2: Won't you join us for a cup of tea?

Wind Woman #1: . . . and a bowl of fresh rice?

Bo: You do eat grains, don't you?

Roe-nye: We are not very hungry.

Tuh-noh: Thank you anyway.

Wind Woman #1: What can we offer you?

Roe-nye: Well, as a matter of fact, you could give

me the secret of love. I ask for it only because I need it quite desperately!

Wind Woman #2 *(pointing to the box on the floor)*: Of course, please take it and enjoy!

★ *ROE-NYE moves toward the box they have been floating around. They surround him, not letting him go.*

Wind Woman #3 *(laughing at how they tricked ROE-NYE)*: Now we have you! And we will never let you go.

Wind Woman #1: We will keep you as our servant.

Wind Woman #2: You will spend eternity catering to our every whim!

Tuh-noh *(pleading)*: No! You must let him go! He is in love. He wishes to marry. Please release him. Let him go and take me! I have no love—except for sushi. I do love sushi.

★ *The WHISTLING WIND WOMEN stop dancing.*

Wind Woman #3: Sushi! We love sushi.

Wind Woman #2: We haven't had good sushi in many, many moons.

Tuh-noh: I have sushi! I never leave home without some.

Wind Woman #1: Then we will make a trade. The boy for your sushi!

Roe-nye: But, Tuh-noh, you love your sushi! You cannot give it up.

Tuh-noh: Here. Take it. Let my friend go free.

★ *The* WHISTLING WIND WOMEN *take the sushi and start to eat it.*

Roe-nye: Tuh-noh, that was very kind. Why did you give away your sushi when you care for it so?

Tuh-noh: I guess that I also care for you—as a good friend. I want you to marry the girl that you love. I think that I am beginning to understand the many different ways that one person can care for another. I care for you as a friend, and Ti-ti loves you.

49

Roe-nye: I also care for you as a friend, and I love Ti-ti.

Wind Woman #2: And we love this sushi! It's great!

Bo: Where did you get this?

Tuh-noh: A little deli on the lower east side of our town. They owe my father money. I can arrange to have some sent to you weekly.

Wind Woman #3: What will it cost us for this service?

Tuh-noh: You must give Roe-nye the secret of love so he can give it to his love, Ti-ti.

All the Wind Women: It shall be done.

★ *Blackout*

Scene 10

★ *Preparing for the wedding.*

Ti-ti *(speaking directly to the audience)*: What great despair! I am not in love with the warrior. I am torn by my dedication to my father and the people of my town and by my own heart. What can I do? If I deny my father, the town might revolt, and I would dishonor my family name. But if I go through with this wedding, I will dishonor my heart and have to live with heartache for the rest of my life. Why must love be so complicated? Why must politics determine my fate? Why must I be a teenager in love?

★ *TI-TI exits.*

★ *BAH-LOW enters.*

Bah-low *(speaking directly to the audience)*: What great despair! I am an honored warrior. I have won many battles and great lands! When will my town allow me to make my own choices? I was

51

forced into this wedding to keep the peace between two towns. Why must I be the bridge between two governments? This is hardly fair. Why can people not learn to settle their arguments among themselves? Every time there is a confrontation I am sent in to fight. This is a battle that I did not choose. I am sure that the girl is kind—but how do I know if I want to marry her? How will I know if I want to marry anyone? Why does it always rain right after I wash my rickshaw? There are so many questions that must be answered!

★ *Blackout*

Scene 11

★ *The whole company is gathered for the wedding.* TI-TI *and* BAH-LOW *stand facing each other on either side of* RUM-TI. KOH-MIE *and* ROE-MAL *stand downstage left. The rest of the company stands in the upstage corners, watching the ceremony.*

Rum-ti *(speaking to the wedding guests)*: As mayor of the town, it is my great pleasure to welcome you to this, the wedding of my daughter, Ti-ti, to the warrior Bah-low from the next town. The marriage will be narrated by Roe-mal and Koh-mie.

★ *Each character bows as he introduces himself.*

Roe-mal: I am Roe-mal, the town cynic.

Koh-mie: I am Koh-mie, the town optimist. It is a beautiful day for a wedding. The sun is shining and the birds are singing.

Roe-mal: Those clouds in the sky may be filled

with rain, and soon we will all be soaked down to our under-kimonos.

Koh-mie: The bride first bows to her groom. Then the groom bows to his bride.

★ *TI-TI bows, then BAH-LOW bows and stays bent over.*

Roe-mal: I hope that his kimono doesn't split when he bends over. That would be so embarrassing.

★ *BAH-LOW stands upright again.*

Koh-mie: The groom must walk around the bride four times to show that he will protect her from the four corners of the world.

★ *BAH-LOW walks around TI-TI four times.*

Roe-mal: I hope he doesn't get lost.

Koh-mie: Now they must share the tea to seal the marriage.

★ *RUM-TI hands a cup to BAH-LOW. BAH-LOW drinks and passes the cup to TI-TI. Before she can drink, ROE-NYE enters with TUH-NOH. ROE-NYE*

carries the box containing the secret of love.
TUH-NOH carries a card.

Roe-nye: WAIT!

Rum-ti: What is the meaning of this?

Roe-nye: This marriage cannot take place! I have been on a journey to find a gift—advised by Tu-bah!

All *(bowing)*: Ah, Tu-bah, Tu-bah!

Roe-nye *(to RUM-TI)*: I have been searching for a gift that would prove to you that I am worthy of wedding your daughter. I have searched far and wide for just the right gift that would express that which is in my heart, and I have found it! I present this to you, Ti-ti. It is the secret of love. I am sure that you know this secret, for I will always be in love with you.

★ *He hands her the box. She opens it and reads the card enclosed.*

Ti-ti: The recipe for sushi à la king.

Tuh-noh: Oh, that's mine! I'm sorry, this must be

yours. *(She exchanges cards with TI-TI.)*

Ti-ti *(reading)*: "Follow your heart."

★ *All bow as TU-BAH enters and crosses downstage center.*

Bah-low *(surprised)*: Tu-bah!

All: Ah, Tu-bah, Tu-bah!

Tu-bah: Follow your heart. That is the secret of love.

Bah-low: That is the greatest gift of all. We can give each other crafts and tokens, but true love is a gift of its own.

Tuh-noh *(to BAH-LOW)*: How did you get so smart?

Bah-low: Everyone thinks that I am a fierce warrior. I have a heart and feelings! I enjoy the oceanside at sunset, the moon on an autumn night, and well-seasoned sushi.

Tuh-noh: You like sushi?

Bah-low: I love sushi! I eat it every day!

Tuh-noh: I love sushi, too!

Bah-low: I'm starving!

Tuh-noh: I know a great little all-night sushi place!

★ *BAH-LOW and TUH-NOH start to leave. RUM-TI stops them.*

Rum-ti: What about the wedding?

Bah-low *(to RUM-TI)*: Sir, your daughter should marry the one she loves. She doesn't love me. She cares for Roe-nye, and I do believe it is the will of your people that she marry the one she loves.

★ *Everyone cheers.*

Tu-bah: You see, the gift of love is more valuable than anything. It is the greatest gift of all!

★ *Ti-ti and Roe-nye join hands. All bow.*

★ *Blackout*

★ *Curtain*

Douglas Love began his career in theater as a child actor and grew up in show business, appearing in more than fifty productions. He has produced five national tours in more than seventy cities across the United States. Mr. Love is the author of *Be Kind to Your Mother (Earth)*, *Blame It on the Wolf*, and *Holiday in the Rain Forest*, all published by HarperCollins. He is also the coauthor of the stage adaptation of *Free to Be . . . You and Me*. Mr. Love is on the faculty of The Children's Theater School in Milwaukee, Wisconsin, and is a guest teacher at the school's Summer Theater Workshop in Vail, Colorado. Douglas Love lives in New York City.